Earnie

My Life at Cardiff City

Robert Earnshaw

ACCENT PRESS LTD

Earnie – My Life at Cardiff City

Published by Accent Press Ltd – 2012

ISBN 9781908192967

The Quick Reads project in Wales is a joint venture between the Welsh Government and the Welsh Books Council.

Printed and bound by CPI Group (UK) Ltd, Croydon, CR0 4YY

Cover design by Madamadari

CYNGOR LLYFRAU CYMRU
WELSH BOOKS COUNCIL

Noddir gan
Lywodraeth Cymru
Sponsored by
Welsh Government

Introduction

I'd like to dedicate this book to my mum and dad. I thank them very much for everything that they've done for me and especially the work my mum did to look after our family over the years.

I remember Oprah Winfrey once said, "I always keep my feet on the ground, it's just now I wear better shoes." I know how lucky I am to be doing something for a living that so many people would love to do. I enjoy everything I've earned and achieved but I know how incredibly fortunate I've been, and I'll never forget the many people, especially my mum, family and friends, who've helped me so much along the way.

Chapter One

THE EARLY YEARS

This may be a startling admission for a professional soccer player to make, but I didn't actually kick a proper football until I was nine or ten.

It wasn't lack of interest. Far from it; as a young child I loved nothing better than a kickabout in the street. It's just that where I was growing up, our 'ball' was rather different to the usual one. It was made of plastic, but not quite the kind you'd imagine. We made our ball by bundling together about twenty-five plastic bags, all scrunched up tight and wrapped around over and over with string. And you'd be surprised how long it would last – we'd play for days and days in the street with our plastic-bag ball. I must make one, just to show people what it was like and how much fun we used to have. I'd be doing my bit for recycling, too!

I was born in Zambia in April 1981, and spent my early years in a place about as far removed from south Wales as it's possible to be.

3

I played barefoot in the playground at school and in the street. We lived in a place called Mufulira, a mining town in the north-west of the country near the copper belt. There are many things I miss about my early life in Africa – the great climate for starters! But most of all, like all of us, I suppose, I miss not having a care in the world. It was a different world over there. My mum Rita had married my dad David, who was originally from Yorkshire and had come over to work in the mining industry. I have a brother, also called David, and sisters Sharon, Joanne and Diane, who is the youngest. Everyone was football mad in Zambia. But it wasn't organised in the way it is in Europe – there was no professional league.

My mum used to play football to a very high level, so the game is in my blood. Also, my cousin and second cousin used to play professionally abroad. One in particular made a big impact and played for PSV in Holland, Cercle Brugge, in Belgium and Club America in Mexico, one of the biggest outfits in South America. His name is Kalusha Bwalya. He was even African Footballer of the Year at one point. His younger brother Joe also played in Belgium. They are both Zambian internationals and Kalusha, who is called 'Great Kalu' by the fans in

Zambia, scored a hat-trick against Italy at the 1992 Olympic Games.

As for my mum, she used to play for a club called Wanderers. She was also a very good boxer – a lightweight – and even sparred against men! But on the football field, she was a prolific goal scorer. I'd watch her matches when I could and I clearly recall the time she came back from a game with a broken leg. I remember how glad we were when her plaster cast was removed.

I was six when we left Zambia to head north for Malawi, where my dad took charge of another mine and we moved to a mining village called Kaziwiziwi. I remember we had a pineapple tree and a banana tree in our garden. Many people grew their own food and we kept chickens, ducks and rabbits.

My dad was very keen for us to get the best education we possibly could, so he got us places at a school six hours travel-time away! It might sound crazy but my dad was keen for us to be taught English and, in Malawi, you couldn't just go to your local school if you wanted that, so it was the best choice as my parents saw it. As a mining engineer, my dad could afford to send us to a private school, although we were far from rich, certainly in European terms. And although the buildings and facilities at the school were very simple, they were a lot better than the schools some of my friends went to. Their schools had earthen floors and no desks or chairs. The toilets were holes in the ground.

There were two of us at the private school, myself and Joanne. It was a boarding school called St Andrew's, and was in a place called Lilongwe. There was no way we could travel daily so we flew, leaving on a Sunday or a Monday and getting back on a Friday. Travelling to school by plane became perfectly normal for us.

It was like so many things in Africa; looking back it's like I've lived in two crazy, different worlds.

I have some good memories of being at that school; I remember one day I lost my schoolbooks and some of the other children teased me that the punishment from the teachers would be being shut in with the school's pet – a crocodile! It was kept on site so you can see how such a threat kept us in line!

I then went on to attend Viphya School, also in Malawi, and by this time I had learned to speak three different languages: Chichewa, which is native to Malawi; Bemba, which is spoken in Zambia, and English. My father spoke to me in English while my mum spoke Bemba and that was my first language. At that age, I guess like all kids, I was a bit like a sponge. I just got on with learning three languages. However, things can change quickly in life and I was to soon end up in a very different country, where yet another language was spoken – Welsh.

Chapter Two

OUT OF AFRICA

Our lives changed beyond all recognition when my father passed away in 1990. He had become ill with typhoid fever and he died in May of that year. I was only nine and it was earth-shattering. It probably seemed best to Mum at the time to move us to south Wales. Her sister Petty and Petty's husband James were already living over here in Bedwas and she had a lot of friends in addition to her sister living here. She'd visited many times over the years.

Looking back, I suppose it's fortunate that I was young and I had my brothers and sisters around me because it was quite an upheaval. I remember finding the weather so cold, and I caught my first sight of snow, which I thought was weird. Mum worked fantastically hard at this time to keep the family going. By British standards we were anything but well off. She took on two jobs and worked around the clock for us. I've got mixed feelings about my life in Africa. It's almost as if my life had started again here. I would like to go back one day, and I do miss Zambia and Malawi. I've never really had the opportunity to return – it's always been my family that has come to us over here. I'd love to take my little boy, Silva, at some stage. However, south Wales was definitely going to come to feel like home and football was going to play a massive part in me settling down here.

I went to school and learned more English but it was in the street that I started my football education. There were rules to the game that I'd never come across before. Even playing with a proper ball was a novel experience. But even at early this stage I got a real buzz from scoring goals. It might have been a kickabout in the road, dodging the traffic, but I just loved scoring.

I attended St Helen's Primary School in Caerphilly first before going on to Cardinal Newman's Comprehensive in Rhydyfelin, and both of these were rugby schools. At St Helen's I did some gymnastics, but nothing serious and although I enjoyed running and athletics, I wasn't good enough to represent the school. I did have a go at rugby at one stage. I think I played full-back and to be honest I didn't have a clue. I just used to run for the try line. There was only ever one game for me – football – but in four or five years I recall us playing only two matches as a school team.

When I was about twelve, a couple of boys I knew who played with the local club said I should come down and join their team. Up until then it had never crossed my mind; I didn't appreciate that there were teams out there that you could just join! Once I joined my local team, which was Llanbradach, I began to enjoy my football even more.

I started out in the under-12 B team. Like anything, it was difficult initially because, apart from one or two boys, they were all strangers to me. But of course it was a good way of making friends. Some of the boys I used to catch a bus to school with were in the team, too, which was great.

As to what position I should play, it was never actually discussed – it just seemed to be accepted that I'd play up front. The first few times I went to training I was just kicking a ball around but word must have got round that I was always scoring goals. People knew that I could do it when playing in the street. I was quite quick as well, so that helped.

It was a well-recognised, established club that had been running for years. I was there for about a year. My mum, with her football background, was interested and pleased that I was playing football and I recall how she'd often watch, even when I was just playing in the street. She would offer encouragement but I didn't need it. Whatever the weather, you'd find me playing football in the street. I was also playing the game at every opportunity in the playground. I think it was all the practice that I was putting in that laid the foundations for my career. Hours upon hours of football. I was playing catch-up, trying to cram in learning the game, the rules and the way everything worked – the kind of stuff maybe kids had learnt at an early age. At Cardinal Newman, every day we'd play for half an hour at break time and then from almost the moment the bell rang for lunch break until it was time to go back in. There were loads of times at dinner break when you'd just be so wrapped up in a game that you'd miss lunch. We'd even get in early in the morning just to start playing before school started. When I did have something to eat at lunch time, I would just dash into the canteen, grab a sausage roll or something, and eat it on the way back out. I'd be running around, with dinner in one hand, playing a match. I never thought twice about it. There would be about twenty-eight of us running around the school yard. It was all very raucous and we took it very seriously. I'd be trying all the time to run through players, taking them on. I used to love going to school, or perhaps more accurately, love going to school to play football! As it's turned out, spending so much time playing has paid off for me, but I'd always say it's best to try hard in lessons, too!

Chapter Three

A TWIST OF FATE WITH TAIT

There are a lot of times in my life where a coincidence or lucky chance has taken me in the right direction. I've been in the right place at the right time. I remember when I first started playing in the street, we'd pick teams to play against kids from one of the other estates and our little team would get talking to the other kids and I got to know a few of them. A couple of them were always playing on a Saturday and a Sunday, and they asked me to join their team. It was called GE Wales, which was effectively the Caerphilly team, and one of the lads in question was Paul Thomas. His older brother was Dai Thomas, who was already a professional footballer and who went on to play for both the Bluebirds and Swansea City. Their dad, Dai senior, was manager of the club.

Playing for Llanbradach had been a great start for me but GE Wales was a different standard. The coaches were excellent and there were a number of very good players in the team. Besides Dai, there was a guy called Phil Williams who did so much to help me, like taking me to training, and giving me lifts. Both Dai and Phil were excellent and they knew a lot about the ins and outs of the game and had us working on pretty advanced stuff for that age and level, like fitness and preparation. It was a very professionally run club and, for under-14s, pretty impressive.

It wasn't long before I was banging in the goals. By the time I was fourteen, I was scoring four or five every game; we were a very strong side. Dai and Phil were very keen for scouts to come down and take a look at us. I was just playing, playing, playing, and to be honest I didn't really take on board what people around me at the club were saying, but I picked up a sense that I was very good. This was the first time I thought seriously about football, and began to realise I might be able to go a long way. Before GE Wales, if you'd asked me what I wanted to be I'd have said 'a footballer' but I didn't have a clue as to how that could happen; I didn't think that a kid like me, who'd been kicking bags around a few years earlier, could even hope to play the game. It was just something that happened on TV, or in a daydream, and nothing more.

Then they started saying at GE that maybe a scout from Cardiff City would be at a game or two. It was all word of mouth, someone trying to sort something out, nothing definite. With hindsight, I should have realised that the people at the club had connections. Then a couple of scouts did come down, one for Manchester United, then a guy from the Bluebirds, and another from Swansea City. There was even talk of me going up to United, but I don't think it was serious. I fractured my shin bone about that time, anyway, so nothing came of it.

I also remember there was someone on the lookout for Oxford United. Again, that was down to Dai and Phil's influence. Me and a few of the other boys were invited over to Oxford. This included Paul, who I played up front with and who, if I'm honest, had a bit more ability than me. We had a try-out for their youth team and it was an eye-opening experience but for whatever reason it didn't go anywhere.

Then something happened which, looking back, was one of the biggest lucky breaks of my life. Being called GE Wales, as people from the area will appreciate, we were sponsored by the factory of the same name and played on the pitches alongside the plant building, which is just outside Caerphilly. They were building aircraft parts and various other bits and pieces and the company was keen to extend out on to the pitches, which meant we'd have to look elsewhere for a venue. Dai and Phil managed to get us moved to the University of Glamorgan pitches at Treforest, near Pontypridd. The pitches and facilities were very good, although it was further to travel. But there was another advantage; we'd been playing and beating most teams in the Caerphilly and district league, but with the move to Treforest we were now into the Cardiff catchment area, which meant we started to play teams from around the city. And even though the standards suddenly got higher, I was still knocking in the goals, seventy-odd one season, in fact.

There was another huge advantage to being at Treforest. Cardiff City's youth side were training and playing there, and on pitches close by. Gavin Tait, who ran the Bluebirds youth set-up, spent a great deal of his time searching for new talent but hadn't realised that there was talent just a pitch or two away, right under his nose! On one occasion we were playing a match on a Saturday morning on the pitch next door to City's youth side and, although I had no idea at the time, we caught Gavin's eye. I remember getting a hat-trick that particular day. In fact I'd played a bit of a blinder, as had one or two of the other boys. After the game he came over to chat to the coaches and mentioned a couple of us. So I got introduced and Gavin asked me to come down to the Bluebirds for training, a bit of a trial really. Again, I remember Dai and Phil telling me how fantastic this was and what a great chance it was, but it still didn't dawn on me that I could be on the road to making it!

Chapter Four

A NIGHT OF ACHIEVEMENTS

The trial had come up in April, a crossroads time; I was nearly sixteen and thinking about what I might want to do for a living. I had some vague ideas, like many kids of that age, and I guess I wanted to do something connected with sport or the game of football. I knew I wasn't the best in the classroom and didn't want to do anything academic. So I was thinking, do I go to Sixth Form, then? But once Gavin Tait had spotted me, I was pretty much finished with school, bar exams. At this point I'd trained once with City, and I was invited to go back a second time. It was to be under the Ninian Park lights.

However, there was a hitch. The night of the second try-out happened to also be Record of Achievement night at school. It was a kind of graduation event and a big night for the family. And here I was, saying to Mum, "Can anyone get me over to training at Cardiff City?" Caerphilly to Ninian Park is a half hour trip, at least. But my mum understood and we decided that we'd try to make the big night at school after the training.

What I didn't know was that the training session at Ninian Park was rather more than just another chance to make an impression. This was the night when the club were going to finalise the Youth Training Scheme (YTS) intake. There were six or so YTS places in total, and at that stage there was only really one place still up for grabs. No pressure then! Luckily, I had no idea what a YTS place was. A YTS place would be the first step on the ladder, a contract with the club which would see you move from triallist to employee, someone the club was willing to invest in.

So, I got a lift over to Ninian Park and it was just a fantastic experience being there that night, playing on the pitch. In the game I did well, really well. At the end, just as I was preparing to dash off to what remained of Record of Achievement night at school, Gavin pulled me to one side and said he wanted a word. He said, "Well done, what we're going to do now is offer you a YTS contract." I was standing there thinking: "So what's that then?" He went on to explain that with a YTS I'd come in every day and train with the youth team. He said the YTS contract would be for two years. I remember thinking, yeh, this is exactly what I want to do. But up until that moment I'd never dreamt that this was something I really could do. So, there I was, having just played under the lights at Ninian Park, a future Cardiff City youth team footballer. But I still had to get to my Record of Achievement night!

Although I was really, really late, I got in just as my class were due on stage to collect our books. Perfect timing, and to say that was one eventful night would be an understatement. But even after being offered the contract, I don't think I really believed I'd become a professional. I was just some kid who'd come from Africa a few years before, and was probably two or three years behind everyone else. But that night at Ninian, the club had selected only me. There were boys who'd been training with City for two years, and yet, after only two training sessions the club had chosen me. It was amazing.

In June that year, I had my first taste of playing for City in a major tournament. We went up to Aberystwyth for the Ian Rush tournament. It's a prestigious youth competition and attracts clubs from all over the world. I was one of the youngest kids there, as most of the players in the Cardiff City team were second year YTS boys. There were only about fifteen of us in the squad, with some of us younger boys just added in for the experience. But I hit the ground running and finished as tournament top scorer, with eleven goals!

During the games I realised that I was with a top, professional club that was known all over the place. It was brilliant to be playing for Cardiff City, and here I was banging in the goals for them. We were there for five days and we lost to Sparta Prague in the final. But I recall a few of the boys in the team saying: "Whoaah, you really know how to score goals." I think I got noticed by a fair few people at that event.

Of course, anyone who has seen me play will be aware that besides goals, I've also got noticed for something else over the years – my trademark somersault. It's something I've been doing since those days back on the pitch at GE Wales and it's got my picture in the papers many times! Well, I did the somersault at Aberystwyth and it was my way of introducing myself at Cardiff City. I remember when I was very young watching football on TV, just loving the goal celebrations. I watched as much as I could, including foreign games, on any channel with football on it. I remember there was a Norwegian guy doing a somersault in one celebration and I thought, I'll try that. I did it for the first time in my first year at GE Wales. I just decided that if I scored I'd do a somersault.

I hadn't practised it, far from it. I just assumed I could do it. I'd done similar stuff in gymnastics at school, which I'd been fairly good at. So I just did it, and there I was, landing back down on my feet! People remember guys like Hugo Sanchez, the great Mexican striker who was scoring goals in the 70s and 80s, for his trademark celebration, but that was more of a hand-spring. What I'd done was a forward somersault and even to this day, I don't think there is anyone else who does quite the same action as me. My favourite celebrators at the time were Ian Wright, Ryan Giggs and Paul Ince and then there was Lee Sharpe, who used to do an Elvis impersonation with the corner flag! I liked that, too. I put my love of crazy celebrations down to being born in Africa, African people love to celebrate! Look at Roger Milla, who set the world alight with his goal celebrations playing for Cameroon at the 1994 World Cup. Bebeto of Brazil, in '94, who did his 'baby rocking' celebration, was another I thought was fantastic.

I know goal celebrations can get players into hot water but I've always seen it as fun, something to put a smile on people's faces. That first time I did it as a fourteen-year-old, I could tell from people's faces that they were pretty stunned and I was told: "Look, you'll break your neck doing that." I knew people were against me doing it, but there was no way I was going to stop. And then, after that tournament at Aberystwyth, people began to think of me as the guy who does the somersault. Some people over the years might have disapproved of my celebration but it was as much a part of my game as scoring goals. Maybe I wouldn't have stood out so much for the likes of Gavin Tait if I'd just celebrated with a handshake!

I must confess, I have messed the somersault up once or twice. I've fallen over at Cardiff and Forest but I've always styled it out so people have thought I meant to go over and then spring up back onto my feet. There has only been one occasion when I've had a real ticking off for it and that was when Alan Cork was the boss at Cardiff City. I remember I'd had a problem with a hamstring and when I came back into the squad, Corky asked me to give the celebration a couple of week's rest but I just couldn't do it. I performed it a couple of times and his response was to hit me with a fine. Well, I say fine; it was £50, which I think he went out and bought a couple of bottles of wine with! He didn't take it too seriously: the one thing that Alan understood was the buzz of scoring goals.

He'd been a striker himself so he could understand the way you just want to jump for joy or, in my case, do the somersault. And after that Aberystwyth trip, I'm happy to say I was doing a lot more acrobatics, as the goals continued to flow.

Chapter Five

BRUSHING UP FOR THE FIRST TEAM

During those first few months as a Cardiff City youth team player, the guys I needed to impress were Kenny Hibbitt, who was director of football at the club, and, in particular, Russell Osman, who was the club manager. It didn't take too long for Russell to start taking a close look at what I was doing, not least because I was scoring in nearly every game I played for the youth side. But I wasn't long for the youth team. I began training with the first team, and spent less time with the youth side. It might have been my first year on a YTS contract, I might have only been sixteen, but I was scoring for fun, often two or three a game. So, as things worked out, that first season at City I scored 57 goals in total for the youth team, trained with the first team and then went on to make a couple of first team appearances.

Just months earlier, I'd been looking ahead to Record of Achievement night at school and wondering what type of course I'd want to do after my GCSEs. To this day, people still ask me how I made such an impact in so short a time. Of course, it wasn't a case of being chucked into the first one day and having your feet under the table straight away. You had to make the right impression for a good few months to feel you were in with a chance of staying. And it was pretty nerve-wracking, suddenly training and playing against men, instead of kids. But the older guys – and some of them were twice my age – had seen plenty of starry-eyed youngsters, and they were all pretty good, joking around, giving us stick. It was the same kind of banter I'd had every day with the youths.

However, there were still things that reminded me, as if I needed reminding, that I was at the bottom rungs of the ladder. Take the chores us YTS lads had to undertake. We all had jobs to carry out at the club – a way of keeping our feet on the ground, I suppose. Some of the boys worked in the boot room, or the tea room, or cleaned out the away dressing room, but my job was to keep clean the home dressing room. We'd watch the first team play or train, they'd finish up afterwards, and then we'd be left to get it back nice and tidy. There was a routine to it that I still know off by heart. We'd sweep up, then take the boots out, mop the floors then dust things down and finally clean the toilets and showers. I did this job virtually every day with a couple of the other lads. On top of that, there were also three sets of boots to clean, but the dressing room was my main chore and while it might sound a bit of a drag, I quickly realised how brilliant a job it was. While other boys were scattered around the stadium doing other jobs, I was always around the dressing room with the first team. It meant that the senior pros got to know my face and bantered with me and it really helped. It was a lot less daunting, when I was in the squad later, than going in to a dressing room full of guys I'd never met. Also, they'd ask me questions about how I was getting on. It was: "How many you scored today, Earnie?" How many goals I was scoring quickly became common knowledge. They'd rib me for only scoring two and not a hat-trick; that kind of thing. Football has changed since those 1998 days and maybe you don't get youth team players carrying out those kinds of chores any more. Young players spend more time on the football and physical side of things. It's more professional. In any case, none of the jobs back then were great, but this particular job was a real result for me. So, when the day came during my first season for me to make my first team debut, the whole experience was a lot less daunting than it could have been.

I remember my debut day well. I'd trained in the morning with the youth and it was a Tuesday, which was always a pretty tough day back then. Next, I got stuck into my jobs, cleaning the dressing room, and cleaning boots, and suddenly Gavin said I was in the first team squad for the game that night against Wrexham in the FAW Invitation Cup. Only after I'd finished my chores, that was! He said there was no point in going home, so I ended up finishing off, sticking on a tracksuit and then going to have a rest. The quietest place was the board room, so up I went and crashed out for a couple of hours and, despite the butterflies and excitement, I managed to grab about twenty minutes of power nap. I was then to meet up with the rest of the squad at 6 p.m. I'd only finished my training and stuff at three! Next thing I knew I was in the home dressing room that I'd just cleaned up, thinking I wouldn't be cleaning it again later! I was on the bench at first, and then with about fifteen minutes to go, I came on. It was fantastic. I've always been grateful for the fact that we had the FAW Cup in the fixture list back then because it gave me my chance.

I then played in an Auto Windscreens Cup game against Millwall in December– only six months after I had left school – and then my league debut came at Brighton, coming on in a goalless draw, on March 28th 1998. I was still only sixteen. Both games were memorable occasions for me. I then achieved another first – scoring my first goal for the club, again in the FAW Cup, against Merthyr. It was all the more special as it was in the second leg of the semi-final, helping us reach the final. I came off the bench and scored the third in a 3-1 win.

But no one was going to let me get too ahead of myself. The three guys whose boots I cleaned were Jeff Eckhardt, Scott Young and Lee Jarman. They had a good mix of experience and know-how. Lee was the joker out of the three, but they all looked after me and as I got more first team, looked after me on the pitch, too. It became normal to be cleaning their boots one minute, then stepping out onto the field of play with them the next!

Kevin Nugent was in the first team when I first came through, as was Steve White and another forward called Andy Saville. Carl Dale and John Williams were two other players who were great to me. All these guys were in their late 20s or early 30s and they were all good at taking the time to teach you the game. When I was on the pitch they'd be telling me what to do and when to do it, when to make a run or when to hold back, what to look out for.

And they weren't shy when it came to putting me firmly in my place. I remember one chat with Steve White very well and I must remind him about it sometime! One day, shortly after I'd scored that first goal in the cup, we were in the gym at Ninian Park. It was a tiny little gym in the back of the stand. I was lifting weights, as was Steve, and he turned to me and said, "Remember, be grateful when you score a goal, because you won't score many of them." I thought that was a funny thing to say because I set high standards for myself. If I didn't score in a game, I'd be gutted. Steve at this point was about thirty, and knew plenty about how careers worked out. So after I told him about how I felt about scoring, he turned back to me and said, "If you get 100 goals in your entire career, I'll give you a £1,000." He wasn't setting a challenge, he just thought it was a safe bet. While it was light-hearted and a bit of fun, he was also serious. At this stage in Steve's career, I'm sure he'd got 100 goals plus, but he'd been around a few clubs and played a lot of games. Steve knew I was young, so I had plenty of time ahead of me, but nonetheless, 100 goals was good going. I thought of what Steve said recently, shortly after I'd scored my 200th goal. I'm about the age now that Steve was then. As I say, I must find out where he lives now and collect my winnings! I'll remind him I was twenty-two when I reached 100 goals!

But the vital thing was that people took the time to tell me how it is. I was a good listener, as I had been as a kid. I've always been a quick learner but I had some fantastic guys around me to help with the steep learning curve. If it hadn't been for them there's no way I would have scored so many goals.

After this initial taste of the first team, things started to happen pretty quickly for me, especially as Frank Burrows then came in as manager. My biggest problem then was people telling me I was too light and too small, and that I'd get kicked around. At the age of sixteen I was only 5 ft 6 in, and weighed 8 st 4 lb. But it didn't stop me scoring. I was getting a hat-trick every game with the youth team. And with Frank Burrows coming in, a lot of players were moved on and at the start of the following season, in August 1998, I found myself making my league debut, and scoring my first league goal.

As league debuts go, mine was pretty fantastic. We were playing Hartlepool away when I found myself in the team for the opening game. It was just such a fantastic feeling. I'd been on the bench and come on during games, but this was my first start in the big time. What was to come was a dream come true. I remember we had a set piece that was half cleared away and then the ball was crossed back in from the right. I didn't see who'd crossed it but it came in behind me and I just did something instinctive. I tried an overhead kick, which nine times out of ten would mean missing the ball, and ending up on my backside. But I connected perfectly and it flew in.

I'd scored some pretty good goals but nothing like this. It was a 'peach' and to get it on my league debut was unbelievable. There was a decent turn-out of Bluebirds fans at the ground that day and they erupted when it went in. It was a perfect moment. I looked at the other guys on the pitch and it was like: "Whooah, what a goal!" It was the perfect way of announcing myself and it made some of the negative stuff on at that time all the more frustrating. Frank, the boss, was an Old School guy. He knew the game inside out but, like so many other people in football, he just couldn't accept that I could be in that first team all the time. I was seventeen, and guys like Frank thought you should hold a seventeen-year-old back. You can't play a lad like that, he's too fragile!

Frank got me doing a lot of gym work and my strength and weight improved, but it wasn't until Frank moved on that I really started to get the sort of lengthy run in the team that I craved.

Chapter Six

THE LOAN RANGER

After hitting that amazing overhead kick against Hartlepool, all I wanted to do was play for my club, Cardiff City. But just a month or two later, I found myself heading off to Middlesbrough for a month's trial. I say trial, but I think in fact it was classed as a loan. I think the reality of the situation was that the club were looking to cash in on me. Remember, this was 1998 and Cardiff City was a club treading water. So, off I went. Looking back now, I think it was a great experience. I'd say I came back wiser. I wasn't against the idea of going, and I didn't have an adviser at the time, so I just accepted it. Bryan Robson was the manager and there were some massive names up there, none more so than Paul Gascoigne. Andy Townsend was also there and it was at a time when their Brazilian superstars, Juninho and Emerson, had just left. I was up there to train with the youth side and also, on a few occasions, join in with first team training.

Being not too far from the likes of Gazza was definitely interesting. I didn't see much of him but when I did spend time training with the first team, you knew he was around! The trial was an eye-opener but then they let me know it wasn't going to lead to anything. So I thought: "Oh, I can go back and play for my proper team, now."

I came back down buzzing, keen to play in the first team. But Frank always seemed reluctant to play me. He was always saying he wanted me to be a little bigger, a little stronger. He was looking after me, really. But in the meantime I was thinking: "I just scored with an overhead kick on my debut, you know?" I felt I could get my experience, and my strength, while I was playing. Besides, I'd always been the smallest. I'd been small at GE Wales, I'd been the smallest and the youngest in the youth team. The same in the reserves. Being small was nothing new and it hadn't held me back, had it?

I was stuck in limbo for another few months until I got to the point when I'd made up my mind to talk to the manager. I had it in my mind to ask about going on loan to another club. I'd had a taste of it, I wanted more. But while I was weighing all this up, Greenock Morton, a club up in Scotland, contacted Cardiff City about me. So Frank sat me down and said, "Listen, I want you to go up to Scotland for three months, you can play some games and get some experience." I was thinking to myself, why can't I do that here? However, I decided, OK, I'll do it. I'll go up there and play. So now I was on my way to Scotland. I didn't have a clue where Greenock was, nor which division they played in. I did a bit of quick research and got up there and went straight into it.

I had digs, a flat with a few rooms above a pub. I know a room above a pub hardly sounds ideal for a sportsman needing his rest, but it wasn't too rowdy, just a very small pub. But I felt a long way from home! The first day I was straight into training, and then just got on with it. I think Frank thought a shipbuilding town like Greenock would be the place to toughen me up. Being Scottish, he knew what he was talking about. There is no tougher place to play than up in Scotland in terms of how physical it is. It was rough, no holds barred on the pitch.

Greenock played in the division immediately below the SPL, the top flight, so it was a decent standard. It did toughen me up but I was already pretty tough. Just to be playing I needed to be tough. I was used to getting kicked. If I spent my time moaning about it, I wouldn't be playing. People were always trying to hack me down but that was their way of trying to stop me doing well and I took it as a compliment. There was plenty of the rough stuff going on when I was up there but luckily I did pretty well. I scored on my debut and I made four starts, with a couple of goals to my name. There was one game when I had to come off at half-time but I hadn't taken a knock – I had a nasty bout of tonsillitis and had spent all the week in bed, from the Monday onwards. I'd felt as if I was dying, and on the Saturday morning I was in the side! I thought: how can I get up, let alone run around in front of 5,000 people? I felt dreadful but in the end I managed forty-five minutes and it was appreciated by everybody.

The highlight of my stay was a game against Rangers in the Cup. Unfortunately, it wasn't at Ibrox: it was meant to be at our ground but it was deemed not big enough, so we played at St Mirren. This was the kind of game I wanted to play in. Rangers had a few of the top Dutch stars with them at the time, Dick Advocaat was manager and Arthur Numan was in the side, as was Giovanni van Bronckhorst. Then there were top Scottish players like Barry Ferguson. I remember thinking the week before that game: this is what it's all about. It was so lucky that my stay there coincided with this game. Andrei Kanchelskis was in the side, too and Tugay had just come over from Turkey. I was playing against top, top players. That team could have done well in the Premier League, let alone the SPL. But from that game, the one player who really stood out was Tugay. I remember coming off thinking: oh my God! He was just amazing, and whenever he was on the ball you could hear a pin drop. I think it was one of his first games for Rangers, if not his debut and he was awesome. But while I was mixing it with Rangers there were major developments back in Cardiff. Frank Burrows resigned and after about a month of being up in Scotland my stay was cut short. Billy Ayre, with whom I'd had a few dealings, took over. Billy had been Frank's assistant and was a more approachable guy and more involved with the youth side of things. I'd had a few chats with him and explained how frustrated I was. Almost as soon as he took over, he brought me back down. And best of all was that I was straight into the first team squad, straight on the bench. It was great, Cardiff was where I wanted to be. Billy was a really nice guy, besides what he did for me. But, looking back, the frustration of loans and being held back was a plus for me in many ways.

Chapter Seven

ALL CHANGE WITH SAM'S CRAZY GANG

If Frank had stayed as manager, I'd have remained in Scotland for at least those two extra months. Or maybe permanently, who knows? But coming back down to Cardiff and getting the kind of opportunities I'd been craving was great. At that time, the club was rather stuck in a rut. This was in the last couple of years of the 1990s and the likes of Sam Hammam, promotion and new stadiums were just pipe dreams. Cardiff City was way off the radar in the wider scheme of things. The club wasn't going anywhere and I could have been sold. Little did we know how things were about to change.

Sam Hammam came in during the late summer of 2000 and brought with him Bobby Gould, the former Wales manager and the guy who led Wimbledon to their famous FA Cup win over Liverpool. Billy went back to being assistant for a while before Alan Cork came in to work with Bobby. I knew Bobby from the Wales youth set-up. He was eventually made a director of football, but while he was involved with training, we had some great laughs. He made the boys feel relaxed. He used to chase me around, grab hold of me and throw me on the floor. The boys I know from that time at Cardiff still talk about it. Me and Bobby would be wrestling on the floor while the other boys were in stitches. It's a good job he didn't injure me!

At that time we were training up in Llanrumney, on the outskirts of Cardiff. For the first fifteen minutes, we'd form a circle, with two boys in the middle. We'd just pass the ball to the boys in the middle and then they'd knock it back to us in turns, and besides warming us up for training, this really warmed up the banter. We'd all be in a relaxed frame of mind, and then Bobby would try and grab me, or go racing after me. I was about twenty, and here I was being chased around a football pitch by Bobby Gould! I think he loved me a bit! He didn't chase anyone else! But, seriously, I'd known Bobby quite well before he'd come to the club and I think he just liked me as a player and as a person. If he liked you, Bobby was a really warm, funny guy. We always got on really well, even if I had to sprint to get away from him sometimes!

After Bobby had moved upstairs, Corky took over as first team boss. He was great for me, as he was a former striker and in many respects was still just one of the lads. He was young to be managing a club and it was perhaps then that we got our first taste of the old Crazy Gang culture at Cardiff City. Like Bobby, Alan was a fun guy who liked us to enjoy our game and to have a smile on our faces. He was brilliant, perfect for our group at the time. The club had been slowly shifting out the older guard and young guys like myself were coming through. We were all developing together and Alan, because of his age and his personality, was the kind of guy we were going to respond to. Laughter and banter suddenly became more noticeable at the club, and to say the whole attitude, the whole ambition changed overnight is a monumental understatement. Sam Hammam had arrived, with his guys, Bobby and Alan, and he had big, big plans for the club.

I remember that first day he came to Cardiff as the new owner. We were all in training and we were told that he'd come and see us afterwards at lunch and introduce himself. Just the usual pleasantries, that's what I'd expected.

However, what Sam did to introduce himself was anything but the usual. He paid a kid a fiver a car to come into the car park and let all our tyres down! Not the tyres on one car, or even a couple. But every single tyre on every car in the car park! So we did our training, finished up, and Sam came in to see us and said how happy he was to meet us. We had a few words, all shook hands and then we got ready to head off. I can't remember who got to his car first but he was really cheesed off because all his tyres were flat. There was no puncture, just four flat tyres, and then the next guy got to his car, took a look at the state of the tyres and realised the same had happened to him. I got to my car and sure enough, four flats. It was, well, crazy.

And that was day one of the Sam Hammam era. It was his unique way of saying: "Here I am, this is what it's going to be like now." Not flat tyres every day, of course, but just crazy. Before he arrived that day, we had no idea if he'd be serious or not. But it was clear that having run Wimbledon in his own unique way, he wanted that to carry on at his new club. He loved all the banter, he loved doing mad things, and he loved all of us wondering what on earth he was going to do next. He kept us guessing from that first day. What was pretty clear was that he wanted to change the whole attitude of the club and wanted to open everybody's eyes to where we could go and what we could achieve. Money was invested in the club, not just in the playing squad, but at all levels. When Sam arrived we were training across the road from Ninian Park, in an open park with dog muck and the rest. He started to gradually change all that.

I've found at all the clubs I've been with in my career that when the right attitude comes in at the very top, you can really go places. It starts at the summit and spreads down to the manager, the players, and the fans. The attitude was: we can do better, a lot better. We can progress upwards.

Right from the very start of Sam being at the club, new and often exciting things were happening. You could see it in the stands. When I first came in to the side, we used to have crowds of about 3,000 or so. It gradually built up and kept pace with the changes that were happening both on and off the pitch. It went from those days of 3,000–4,000 to 17,000 and then more, as it is now in the new stadium. We were filling Ninian Park on a regular basis.

We had some big occasions. We were promoted a number of times, and we had some huge cup games, like against Leeds, who at the time were at the top of the Premier League, in the FA Cup. We got to the point where we were averaging 12,000–13,000 crowds, and there are plenty of big city clubs around who'd be envious of that kind of regular support, I loved that time at the club. It was very exciting and anything seemed to be possible. We were developing as players, and the club was going in the right direction at last.

Chapter Eight

OUR PREMIER PASSION

The business models of most of the teams around us, certainly in Division 3 (League One as it is now) and to a lesser extent Division 2 (the Championship now), was focussed on survival, and getting by as best you could. But ours now revolved around one question: how can we get promoted? I know Sam Hammam fell out of favour with the fans, and there was a lot of anger and a great many people in Cardiff still have very mixed feelings about him. But overall, I think fans have a lot to be grateful for. Sam gave the club something it had not had before, or at least not for many years: a vision. He said, "Why can't we play in the Premier League?" People may have found that a crazy idea but he'd played a big part in helping Wimbledon fly up through the divisions, so he had the drive and the ambition to take a club somewhere.

There are many arguments about what Sam did and didn't do, but I'm convinced Cardiff City would not be where we are today without his involvement. We're a Championship side and without wishing to tempt fate, we're an established Championship side and it's unlikely we'll go any lower than that. I remember that before Sam came to Cardiff City people talked of us as a sleeping giant. But I think Sam was the guy who really bought into that idea. He could see the potential here. OK, it's the manager and the players who win games, not the owner or the chairman, but he helped give us the tools, at least at the start. Money was spent, and he made sure that the resources were there to improve us and not to just keep us ticking along.

But for me there was another, key ingredient. He helped make Cardiff City a fun, enjoyable place to be. Everybody in Cardiff, Wimbledon, and throughout the game knows a few stories about how *different* Sam was. When we signed Spencer Prior, a player who cost the club a lot of money and turned out to be an important signing for us, Sam inserted a clause into his contract saying that he had to eat sheep's testicles. Perhaps he thought it would prove Spencer was a man! But Spencer wanted to sign and I believe he did it. Sam took him to a restaurant and they were served up for him. Maybe it was a more of way of being certain a player really wanted to join! Even now, I thank the Lord that he never asked me to eat sheep's dangly bits!

I signed lots of contracts while he was at Cardiff. In one year I think there were four. And each time I was thinking: is he going to get me this time? You were checking to see that he hadn't slipped in a clause about having to do a bungee jump in your boxer shorts at half-time, or something like that. But I got away with it though Spencer and a few others had to undergo some bizarre challenges. He was, and I'm sure still is, unique. However, on the pitch we played the proper way. We were deadly serious when we played, but it was a laugh a minute when we weren't playing. One particular Sam moment stands out in my memory more than any other. He was always talking about trying to make us a Welsh team, trying to make us the club the whole country could support, and a big part of that was having a lot of Welsh players in the team. So we had quite a few lads in the Wales under-21s and on one particular trip three or four of the boys broke a curfew, went out when they shouldn't have, and got thrown out. I was injured, so I wasn't there. But I was called into a meeting with Sam on the Monday, despite not being involved in what had happened. And I was thinking: why am I here? I've done nothing wrong. So I went into the room and all the boys were there staring at the carpet. I kept telling myself that I was in the clear. But I thought maybe somebody was going to get the sack.

Sam was pacing up and down, shaking his head, looking stern and we were all sweating, waiting for a right old rollicking to start. Lennie Lawrence was in the room, too, which suggested this was very serious. Sam broke the silence and I think he just said, "I'm disappointed." I remember thinking: I'm glad I'm not involved in this, I can just sit here. But then after a moment's silence he suddenly clapped his hands together and said, "OK, that's enough of that. I'm glad you did what you did, I'm glad you did it, I'm proud of you. We can't all live a straight life, we can't all be goody goodies all the time. Sometimes we make mistakes but I'm really proud of you all." He said all that, with a quite a few swear words thrown in, and then the whole room erupted in laughter. That was Sam to a tee. Anything was possible.

I remember a lot was said about how Sam might have made a mistake that famous day we played Leeds in the Cup, and he walked around the pitch and the fans were chucking stuff at him and there was nearly a riot. But my attitude is that, it was Sam's club, and if that's what he wanted to do, well, it might be crazy and it might have been a mistake, but that's what he wanted to do. I've certainly never been at a club with an owner or chairman like Sam. What it all boiled down to was that he believed people might get it wrong here and there, but what mattered more than anything was being together. He was loyal. Sam knew the lads who'd stepped out of line on that Wales trip were good boys. He was like a father bringing his children back into line. We came out of that meeting thinking he was amazing.

The club really looked after the players. Everybody was happy, there was no one with a gripe. It's why I stayed for seven and a half years. It was an enjoyable place to be.

Sam was also so involved. People saw him sitting in the dug-out. How many club chairmen do that? In the dressing room, for example, you'd have Bobby Gould there as director of football, and Alan Cork as manager, and Sam would be in there with them. It was normal. He'd have a note pad and he'd listen to the team talk with us and write it all down, all the instructions we were getting, about set pieces, who was marking whom, that sort of stuff. He'd then be watching to see if we did what we'd talked about, I suppose.

I remember one particular occasion when

we'd just lost to Reading. We got back into the changing room and the manager, I think it was Lennie Lawrence at that time, started going through what had gone wrong. Sam just stood in a corner listening and then suddenly broke in with his own take on it. I remember him saying that they should have had a guy sent off and he told us exactly how he'd seen it, what we should have done and where we hadn't listened to the team talk. Now, a fair few club chairmen will come into the dressing room afterwards and have a quick word but Sam was right in the thick of it. Look at some of the guys who own the big Premier League clubs these days, they might go and watch their club a couple of times a season. But Sam Hammam, love him or loathe him, was always involved. He'd be on the team coach with us, or staying in the same hotels on the away trips. He was always very, very hands-on. Nothing was ordinary, everything was out of the box, but we were all part of one big, wonderful family.

Chapter Nine

A PERFECT SEASON

Every player around the world must have a favourite season, one when everything seems to fall in your favour. A season to remember and look back on when you're old and grey. It's fair to say I've always contributed goals during my time at Cardiff City, but the 2002–3 season, which was our second in Division 3 (now League One) following promotion in 2001, was pretty special, both for me on a personal level and for the club. It is without doubt my favourite season and you'd have to go some way to top it.

I recall pre-season had gone pretty well but I started the season on the bench. I was still young, in my early 20s, so perhaps I was still expecting too much. But my attitude was, right, I've got a couple of seasons around the first team under my belt, so I should be in the first team. We started the season with Andy Campbell, a striker who'd come in from Middlesbrough, and Peter Thorne, the club's most expensive signing at the time, as the main guys up front. Plus a striker called Leo Fortune-West was still strongly in the picture, so I found myself behind these guys, even though I'd scored in the opening game of that season, which was against Oldham.

We went about seven or so games into the season like this, with me thinking I should be playing, and my family, friends and anyone biased in my favour, thinking: "Why is Earnie not playing?" In the end, though, it was manager Lennie Lawrence's call and I trusted his judgement. He was, and always will be in my mind, a great manager. So although I did question him, I also respected his decision. It was just frustrating.

Then in the second week of September we had a League Cup game against Boston United. Lennie decided he wanted to change things around and he told me I'd get a start. I scored a hat-trick in a 5–1 win. I came off the pitch that night thinking to myself: so, are you going to play me now? I'm thankful that I didn't let the boss down. During the next six league fixtures I scored eight goals. It seemed that whoever we played against, I'd get a goal or more. The nucleus of the team at that stage had been together for two or three seasons and we knew each other well. Crucially for me, this was a team that was always creating chances. I just loved playing in that team. It was a dream come true for a striker, because the supply line always delivered up more than enough chances for me and the other boys up front to provide the goals.

Also, this was the season when Thorney and I really clicked. Peter was bigger than me, and I suppose you could say we were the traditional big man – little man combination up front. But Peter was far more than just a target man or foil for a little goal scorer like me, he was a real predator in front of goal in his own right. I think this was the key. Instead of us having different strengths that complemented each other, we both thought the same way. We understood each other because he was a goal scorer, and so was I.

So we found that from the September onwards we developed an almost telepathic partnership on the field and became established as the first choice pair up front for the club. We'd always be looking for each other. We created chances for each other and scored goals. I knew what he wanted, and vice versa. We knew the kind of runs we'd make, I knew where he wanted the ball and he knew where I wanted it. We had a superb level of intelligence within the partnership. From playing alongside Peter I learned a lot about building a partnership with another striker, stuff that I've taken forward in the later stages of my career.

One thing that sticks in my mind from 2002–3 is that once I got into my stride, I seemed to score just about every time I touched the ball. I kept thinking: is this really happening? I felt like pinching myself because none of it seemed real. I had a run of nine, maybe ten games when I scored goal after goal and it seemed almost too good to be true. The run started after that Boston game and I never looked back. So much so that it was quite early in the season that people started to talk about breaking goal-scoring records. I got up to about twenty-two or twenty-three goals and it wasn't that long after Christmas. I pushed all those thoughts to the back of my mind. I was too busy scoring goals! Then I got up to twenty-seven and there were still a fair few weeks of the season to go. So then rewriting the record books at the club started to become something I thought I could do and something I really wanted to achieve. I don't remember feeling any additional pressure, it was just something I wanted to do. At the time, the bigger question, by far, was: are we going to get promoted? We'd been in and around the top six of Division 3 but by the time we got to the business end of the season, it looked like it was probably going to be the play-offs for us. By the last fortnight, it was confirmed that automatic promotion was going to be beyond us.

We played a big game against Tranmere Rovers, who included our current physiotherapist, Sean Connelly, in their side. It was one of the last games that season and I scored a hat-trick to break the league goals record, one that had stood since Stan Richards had hit thirty in the 1946–7 season. It was great for me. But we finished up drawing the game 3–3, which despite Tranmere being a very decent side, was still frustrating as we needed to gain as many points as we could. I remember scoring with just about the last kick of the game to equalise.

After the game Lennie, the boss, singled me out, which was really nice of him, and congratulated me on breaking the league scoring record, but made it clear that we'd defended very badly. There were a lot of mixed emotions that night. I was halfway to breaking two records that had stood for seventy-five years, but we also knew we'd have to battle to get promotion.

So, it came down to the last game of the season proper, a game against Crewe at their Gresty Road ground. At this stage I'd scored thirty goals in the league, thirty-four in total and I was one away from breaking the all-time club goal-scoring record set by Hughie Ferguson in 1927. Now, with the play-offs being the overriding priority for the club, one or two of the players had been rested by the boss with an eye to making sure people were fit and ready for the play-off semi-finals and then hopefully the final. Lennie and I had a conversation. I kind of knew what was coming because the emphasis had shifted from the league campaign to the lottery of the end-of-season play-offs. He said, "Look, Earnie, I know you need a goal to break a record but I've got to think about the play-off games and I'm going to rest you. You'll probably get on against Crewe at some stage but you're starting on the bench."

There'd been so much said about the records, the one for the league, which I'd broken, and then the one for all competitions. But the bigger picture was, well, bigger than me and records. Trouble was, I wanted it all. I wanted promotion and to play against Crewe, to get the record, and to play the next week. I wanted to break the record because it was impossible to imagine having another season like this, so it would be my one and only chance. I just needed one goal, and scoring in the play-offs wouldn't count. It had to be in the season proper. But the club needed promotion.

So there I was, on the bench at Crewe, bobbing up and down from the first minute, just longing to get on the pitch! It was pure agony. A few chances came and went and I was thinking: "I could have got on the end of that!" I don't think I've ever felt quite so frustrated. At half-time, one of the longest halves of my life, we were a goal down. I got back on the pitch during the interval to get warmed up – I don't think it's possible for anyone to have been more enthusiastic about a few stretches! It kept going round, over and over in my head: "This is the last game, this is my last chance." Would I get ten minutes? Maybe half an hour? If we scored an equaliser, would I get on at all? I feared the record would stand for another seventy-five years. I think Lennie got the message, since it was written all over my face. I could have kissed him when he said I was coming on right at the end of the half-time break. Now I had my chance. I'd actually had a T-shirt printed with the word 'boom!' on it, to show to the fans in the event of getting on and scoring. 'Boom!' was the word of the season for us at Cardiff City – it came from playing cards on the bus going to away games, and you said it when you'd got a winning hand and pretended to shoot the pot. We'd even spoken about it to the press.

So it was now down to me to take a chance. I didn't try shooting from the halfway line, or do anything daft, but every time I had got the ball someone shouted shoot! All the fans knew what was at stake and they were great, willing me to do it. And then it came, one clear chance. I was put through one-on-one with the goalkeeper. I don't even remember who played me in, I was just there and boom! I slipped it through the keeper's legs. I whipped off my shirt to show the T-shirt underneath. I felt amazing. I was so happy to have beaten the record and the circumstances were just perfect.

It was an incredible feeling to have scored thirty-five goals in a season, one more than any other player in the history of Cardiff City. A couple of weeks later, of course, we managed to cap even that. We got to the play-off final, which by fate happened to be in Cardiff, at the Millennium Stadium. There we beat QPR and sealed our place in the Championship for the next season. It was an incredible, emotional day. Thirty-odd thousand Cardiff fans, everyone deliriously happy, and we were a step closer to everyone's dream of one day reaching the Premier League. You couldn't have asked for anything more.

Chapter Ten

MY STAND-OUT CARDIFF GOALS

This might surprise people, but a lot of games I've played and goals I've scored have become a bit of a blur in my mind, simply because I've had so many good moments. I am very lucky to be a player who has scored a lot of goals, more than two hundred and still counting, touch wood. But some of those goals have really stood out for me, either because of the occasion, or because they were spectacular in some way.

I'd say my favourite goal, in terms of how eye-catching it was, and who I scored against, is one that I got against Stoke City at Ninian Park in November 2003. It was a game we won 3–1, a good performance all round. The goal was a volley, from a header from one of our midfielders at the time, John Robinson. I was twenty-five yards out, maybe further, and I just struck it as well as I could. Ed de Goey was in goal – a top-class Dutch international at the time – and it was particularly satisfying because the way I caught it didn't give him much chance. It's great to score eye-catching goals like that, and I recall the first half of the 2002–3 season being a time when I scored a fair few top-draw goals, which gave me and the team a lot of satisfaction.

We played a game against Colchester during the week before Christmas in 2002. It was an away match at Layer Road, which is never the easiest place to get a result. We won 2–1, and I remember one of my two goals that day as another real favourite. Our goalkeeper, Neil Alexander, kicked downfield and then Peter Thorne got a touch on it. The ball came out to me way over on the left and I just remember glancing up and seeing their keeper was off his line. I hit it first time. The keeper had no chance, even from that angle and that distance. It was just a perfect finish and I know the fans enjoyed it.

People ask me about how I get my goals. Goals like that, in fact probably about 70 per cent of all the goals I score, are largely down to pure instinct. However, I do try to pre-plan the odd goal. Sometimes I've had a particular kind of goal in mind for a while, one that I want to score, and what was particularly satisfying about that goal at Colchester was that it was the kind of finish I'd been thinking about for a while. I fancied scoring something spectacular from long range and maybe a tight angle, and this proved to be the perfect moment to score it. It was the right place, right time.

There are two others that spring to mind from a little earlier in that same season. One was against Crewe at Ninian Park in late September. We were a goal down for much of the game until I scored two in the last five minutes to turn the game on its head. First I got the equaliser and then, for the winner, I think Leo Fortune-West nodded down for me. I had my back to goal, but turned and smashed it away, and it was a fantastic feeling. We'd snatched victory from the jaws of a defeat. It underlined the fact that the confidence in the team was just so good.

Then, a week later, we played Wigan in a 2–2 draw at the JJB Stadium up there. This was another game which said a lot about our confidence and ability. I'd scored in the first half but we found ourselves 2–1 down in the second, with time running out. I think the ball came in from the left, Graham Kavanagh cushioned a little header in for me, and I flicked the ball over my shoulder, turned and struck it just right. Wigan were a well-established side in the division and again it underlined the feel-good factor for us that we'd gone there and given them such a good game.

Besides the part that instinct plays in the game of a goal scorer, there are other skills that over the seasons I've honed and developed. One thing I've always tried to do, if this doesn't sound too cosmic, is to predict the future. What I mean is that I gamble on where I think the ball is going, where I think the defender or keeper may go, and also on the kind of position I need to be in to take the chance that may be coming. I'm always trying to second-guess the future. I want to be three, four or even five steps ahead and you can put yourself there by anticipating correctly what is about to happen. From experience, you develop a fine instinct for this kind of anticipation. You learn to read situations.

Of course there are many times when things don't go as you predict and times when you miss. But that's OK – it's not possible to score every goal on offer. The goal against Colchester was one I'd already played out in my head and the key is to be in the position to take the chances. The great players that I've watched closely all do this. My big heroes have included Romario, Ronaldo, Eric Cantona, Diego Maradona and Juninho, and they've all been great at getting into the right positions. I've never worried about how many goals I'm going to score, it's always the number of chances I'm going to get that concerns me.

I used to think I was the only guy who thought like this. But then I remember listening in to a conversation John Hartson was having, I think during a Wales trip. It was years ago, when big John was still at Celtic and he was talking about the great Henrik Larsson, who, for me, is a god at the art of scoring goals. Larsson scored goals from close range, from distance, with his head, and with both feet. He has just been a goal machine and he's the kind of player I've looked at closely because, as I've said, you try to pick up things from other players' games and Henrik is a player anyone can learn from. The conversation turned to what Larsson did that makes him so special, and John said that the one thing he did that mattered more than anything was that he got himself so many chances. He's not the kind of guy who waits for something to happen, he makes things happen, and that's what I mean by gambling and trying to anticipate.

When John said this it really clicked with me – it was exactly the way I thought. And it made me feel that my approach was the right one. When you are young and want to improve, you get as much bad advice as good. But that is what helps you be a better player. It's not just all about practising on the pitch, but also listening and learning. And if you worry about taking your chances, then you're in the wrong game. It's making sure you get a chance, and working with others who will give you that chance, that counts.

As for other goals that stand out for me, I recall one against Northampton when I scored the type of goal people the world over love to see, an overhead kick. As a kid I loved practising overhead kicks. I wanted it to be my speciality. I'd got that one against Hartlepool and in this game at Northampton, in early 2003, I scored another, albeit from quite close in. I've never been keen on the idea of being bracketed. Some strikers are known as target men, others goal-poachers. I've never wanted to be a certain 'type'. I've always wanted to show a range of qualities as a player, and to try different types of goals, and different types of finishes from different positions and angles. Sometimes, what you achieve is influenced by the kind of team you're in, but at that stage of my career with Cardiff City we were pretty free-flowing. For this goal, a cross came in and Thorney thundered a header against the bar and I just went for it, jumped and hooked in the overhead on the rebound. They always look spectacular and I'm glad to say that I've got that kind of finish in my locker.

Another goal that ranks high for me came much later that same year, against Burnley at Turf Moor. It was November and we drew the game 1–1, which was no mean feat at the time, and I scored a cracking goal even though I was actually pretty unwell on the day.

The evening before the game when we arrived at our hotel I was fine, but in the night I'd started to feel a bit rough and by the morning I'd got a thumping headache and felt rubbish. It's always been my habit to miss breakfast on the morning before a game and to lie on in bed and have a rest before getting moving about 10.30 a.m. But even with the lie-in, I felt pretty dreadful. So I went down for our pre-match meal and told the physio how I felt, although because I was so keen to play, I wanted to wait until we were getting on the bus to head off to the ground before making a call on whether I'd play or not. As kick-off got nearer, I resolved to play, although I don't think I was feeling that much better. But it was a good job I made the extra effort because I hit a superb 25-yarder with my left foot which helped to secure a point. I remember thinking after it had gone in: "How have I just scored that?" I have to say it made me feel better, though only slightly, and I think I was packed off as soon as possible. I think I remember that goal all the more because of how rough I felt.

Going a little further back, I remember one of the hat-tricks I scored for the club very well because this happened the first time I captained Cardiff City. I took great pride in being captain. We were playing a Carling Cup fixture against Leyton Orient in 2003 and I think quite a few of the first team guys were rested or unavailable. At that time, Graham Kavanagh or Andy Legg would have been the skipper but neither were playing so the armband was up for grabs. I remember we were all sitting around the dressing room, and Lennie at that point hadn't named the team, let alone the skipper. There was a lot of banter about who'd get the armband and a few of the lads were jokingly putting my name forward. Lennie was involved in the conversation and I said, "Yeh, give it to me, I'll have it." There was probably quite a lot of mickey-taking, because I was only twenty-one at the time but I'd been at the club since the age of sixteen and had been around Ninian Park longer than pretty much anyone, so I suppose I felt like I deserved the chance. Lennie took a bit of convincing but I said I wanted to be captain, and in the end he gave it to me. I don't know if it was due to taking on the extra responsibility, but I scored a hat-trick in just seventeen minutes! One of the three goals was particularly nice. I managed to chip their keeper into the far corner. I think the armband suited me!

I remember getting out on the pitch and shouting a bit more, thinking I've got to lead by example but in all honesty being captain is just a symbolic thing. It's an honour to be asked to do it, but it is just an armband, at the end of the day. After the game, there was quite a bit said about how I could be a lucky captain and maybe I should keep the armband. But Kav and Leggy would have had something to say about that!

While that was my first hat-trick as skipper, my first hat-trick ever had come a few years earlier, in 2001, against Bristol Rovers in a televised game. Hat-tricks have come along quite frequently; I've been lucky – I seem to have had the knack of being able to get a goal and then quickly add more, so much so that I'm the only player to have scored in all four divisions, in the regular cup competitions and for my country. But this Bristol Rovers game was when people beyond Cardiff City really first started to be aware of me. It was on Sky TV, so it was like saying to the world: "I'm here, this is me."

Fast-forwarding to September 2003, there's one more game that sticks in my mind because of the goals I contributed. Some days just about everything you touch goes in and that was certainly the case during this game we played against Gillingham. It stands out for two reasons, the first being that I scored four goals, apparently it was the first time in thirty-two years that a City player had got that many in a league match, and also because my mate and fellow Wales international Jason Brown was in goal for them. I must admit that we gave him a bit of a nightmare that day, although you couldn't have blamed him for our 5–0 win. We were just right at the top of our game that day. I'd had a quiet spell in front of goal leading up to it, so I was up for a few goals. The chances just came along and it was: bam, bam, bam, bam. To get four chances in a game, let alone four goals, is good going but the beauty of the team we had then was there were so many good, creative players in the side who could open things up for me and others. I remember Jason's face. He must have been thinking: "Not another one!" But I don't think I could have been enjoying my game more! I came off the field with a huge grin on my face and the match ball under my arm!

Chapter Eleven

GAME FOR A LAUGH

There have been some great characters at the club in the time I've been at Cardiff City, but one or two players and a few incidents stand out.

One of the funniest guys I've ever played with was a lad called Andy Jordan, a defender and the son of former Scotland international Joe Jordan. He was around for a while during my first couple of years in the first team and he was someone you had to watch like a hawk. He was always up to something and his speciality was cutting up shoe laces. He loved practical jokes, and I remember one day sticking my foot in my trainer in the dressing room and finding it had been filled with red sauce. I knew exactly who to blame.

Around about that time Leo Fortune-West came to the club, and he was on the receiving end of plenty of stick. He was a really big, tall guy, about 6 ft 5 in, but his legs were a bit weird. It was as if he had no calves. We asked him, "Who's nicked your calves, Leo?" and he had to put up with jokes about his calves for years. Also, when he spoke, you couldn't believe his voice. He was a massive guy, but his voice sounded like that of a funny little boy! He was very softly spoken and he looked like an accountant, very business-like and clean cut, always neat and tidy. It was a red rag to a bull for us. We took the mickey and to be fair he went along with the banter and gave us some stick back. Leo was a good laugh.

As for stories, I remember one about a Dutch player we had at the club right at the start of my career, called Winston Faerber. Winston was a big defender and he'd just arrived at the club. We were on an away trip and the club physio told him to have a swim, a sauna and a session in the jacuzzi, just to relax and wind down. Apparently, although I didn't witness this myself, Winston came out of the changing rooms with a towel wrapped around him and then, just before going into the sauna, hung up his towel to reveal he was without trunks. In fact, totally naked! He then went into the sauna, which already had three or four people in it. They all got out sharpish and left Winston to it, he didn't realise that going into a public sauna naked in this country is not really the done thing. I think he might then have got in the pool. The boys who saw all this were in stitches but before there was a serious complaint somebody told him he needed to cover up. He was pretty embarrassed!

Graham Kavanagh, who came to the club a few years later, was skipper for a time and he told me something that I was really surprised at. Kav came to Cardiff for a big transfer fee and was a superb player, with plenty of experience. I remember one day him saying, "Remember, there are people here who look up to you." It seemed a funny thing to say to me when I was still in my early 20s, but he told me and my mate Danny Gabbidon this and it stuck with me. I hadn't thought of such a thing before and it was good advice. He was always telling us to be professional and remember to do the right things. Mind you, I think we returned the favour by taking the mickey out of Kav's hair! He was pretty grey up top, even though he wasn't old.

But while the old guys were great, my biggest pals at the club were those closer to my age group, boys like Josh Low, Gabbidon, James Collins and then, later on, Joe Ledley. James has been one of my really good mates for years. He's a bit younger than me and I first came across him when I played a couple of youth team games, despite having been involved with the first team, just to keep my fitness up. James, or

'Ginge' as he's been known for years, stood out. I think he was louder than everyone else! He was quickly involved with the first team and just fitted in, and despite the fact that we've moved in different directions over the years, we're still really good mates.

It was much the same with Joe, who came through into the first team not long before I was moving on. I remember Lennie Lawrence brought him in to first team training and he took to it like a duck to water. You could see he was going to be a top player. We didn't even know his name, but he was so confident; he seemed to know exactly what to do and when to do it. I gave him a nickname pretty quickly, though. I started calling him Bruce Lee! His hair was longer at the back and he looked a bit like the kung fu legend. We all had a good laugh and maybe the banter helped him settle into the squad. He has gone on to do very well.

Chapter Twelve

ON THE MOVE

For about a decade, it has been my dream, my overriding ambition, to play for Cardiff City in the Premier League. It's an ambition that was sparked by Sam Hammam's arrival at the club and, for a couple years at the start of the last decade, it was a dream I genuinely thought could be realised. But by 2004, things were starting to change at Ninian Park. The free-spending days of Sam's early years at the club, when all that mattered was driving the club up through the divisions, regardless of the financial impact, were about to come to an end.

And I'm sure that it was because of this more realistic approach to the club's bank balance that I found myself swiftly and dramatically exiting the club I so loved being a part of. When I'd first broken through at Cardiff City, and even before that, as a sixteen-year-old, Cardiff had been a selling club. But Sam had gone a long way to changing all that. From about the start of the decade onwards the local media often linked me with moves to this or that club, but it all went straight over my head and a bullish Sam Hammam would make some comment about how I was not for sale. At no point did I want to move, regardless of the clubs being bandied around. OK, I did occasionally think it would be nice to play for one of the really big clubs but what I wanted more than anything was to be at the highest level with the Bluebirds. We'd gone up through the divisions, and we were now in the Championship. Anything seemed possible.

But by 2004 the mood had altered. The club wasn't spending money on players the way it had been. And during that summer there were rumours, talk that players might really be leaving, to balance the books. It wasn't anything concrete, and all I wanted to do was get stuck into playing for Cardiff because I believed we were on the verge of reaching the Premier League. I believed it was going to be a big season for me at the club, maybe the biggest so far, and we would be there in the promotion push.

But then, at the end of August, we played a League Cup game against Kidderminster. It was a night match and we were in the dressing room and someone said that a guy from a Premier League club was going to be in the crowd watching me. How that was public knowledge I don't know, but I decided to ignore it and got on with getting ready. But then I was out on the pitch warming up and one or two of the boys told me that Gary Megson, the West Bromwich Albion manager, was in the stand to watch me. I thought, oh, that's cool, but it didn't really register with me as anything particularly serious. My attitude was then, and always has been, that unless something is concrete I'm not going to worry about it.

Anyway, the game started, I scored, and the tie went to penalties. Again, I scored in the shoot-out but I wasn't trying to impress anyone, I was just doing my job. We won through the tie and that was that. I didn't give it another thought until a week or so later when, after a training session, Lennie said he wanted to see me in his office. Now, if you're called into the boss's office after training, you're either in big trouble, or you're about to be offered a new contract. Before I went in to see Lennie, I'd convinced myself it must be about a new contract because as far as I could see, I hadn't stepped out of line in any way. So I went in and sat down and Lennie got to the point. He said West Bromwich Albion had offered £3.5 million for me. He added that the offer had been accepted. My response was just: "Oh, right." Although I was still pretty young, I had quite a good head on my shoulders and I wanted to let this news sink in a bit before I said anything. Then Lennie asked me what I wanted to do. It was dawning on me that Lennie had been quick to point out the offer had been accepted. He asked again what I fancied doing and I suppose at that moment the writing was on the wall. What I wanted to do was stay at Cardiff City. What I wanted was to play in the Premier League with Cardiff City. I didn't want to leave. But in the end my agent spoke to West Brom and the feedback was that they really wanted to sign me. I started thinking about it then; this was an offer to play in the Premier League. An offer was on the table. I was torn, really, really torn. I asked myself over and over, what should I do? What was clear was that the club wanted to sell. They needed money – otherwise they would not have accepted an offer. In the past, the club's stance had been that they wouldn't sell unless it was really crazy money. That had clearly changed. So I spoke to West Brom. This was all happening right at the end of the summer transfer window. The clock was ticking to get everything done before the window shut and no more transfers could go ahead until January. While discussions were on-going with Albion there was suddenly also talk of a move to Everton. They began speaking to my agent and we had to weigh it all up. I remember we were actually en route to West Brom for further talks when the Everton offer kicked off, though despite there being conversations, nothing was being formally offered. It was a race against time to get everything done and Everton, who were an interesting possibility for me, in the end appeared to be just messing us around. I had to make a decision and so, after talking to West Brom, I signed for them.

It sounds so easy but, honestly, it was about the hardest decision I've ever made. Even after I'd signed for West Brom, I didn't want to leave. I went back to Cardiff City to pick up my stuff, and I saw the lads and they all said they hoped it went well for me and goodbye, that kind of stuff. But I still didn't want to leave. I felt pretty emotional. I hadn't had the chance to say any kind of farewell to the fans. The City fans had meant so much to me over the seasons I'd been at the club. They'd backed me and supported me through thick and thin and the last thing I wanted to do was turn my back on them and disappear off somewhere else. If I had to go, I wanted time to say goodbye. At the same time I was thinking that if I had to leave, it had to be for the Premier League, and this was what was happening. But the truth of the matter is that the club really took the decision out of my hands. In football, as in other sports, you can ask to move to another club. But unlike other walks of life, in football you can just as easily have the rug pulled from under you and be told your club has agreed to sell you. It can be very harsh. I realise fully just how fantastic it is to be a professional footballer, but when a club decides to cash in on you, it means uprooting your family and starting again, whether you like it or not. That isn't easy to do and some players have to do it a few times in their careers.

However, this move was the chance I'd dreamed of to play against the likes of Manchester United and once I'd taken a look at West Brom's fixtures, I started to be more positive about what had happened. I'd signed for Albion and my debut was going to be against Liverpool, at Anfield, no less. Playing at Anfield is a dream come true for any professional player. It doesn't get any better than that. This was the highest level. My mum and my family were all being as supportive as they could be. Mum didn't want me to leave. It's tough on any mum when their kids move away but she was really happy for me that I was going to be playing in arguably the biggest league in the world. The family were all behind me because they really wanted to see me in the Premier League.

One thing that probably made this sudden turn of events easier to handle was that it all happened so quickly. We didn't have time to agonise over it. It was bang, bang, bang, deal done.

Although it was a shock, I certainly don't blame the club for how things turned out. They needed money and a good offer was there. It was a choice for the good of the club. Lennie wasn't in a position to try to influence me; he had to work in the club's best interests, though I'm sure he would have liked to tell me to stay with Cardiff and turn West Brom down. But if I had turned West Brom down, what would have happened then?

The next thing I knew I was in the tunnel at Liverpool with my new team mates, touching that famous "This is Anfield" sign and walking into the away dressing room, which is a little way down that tunnel and on the left, by the way. And everything that had happened started to make a little more sense to me after that game, as I swapped shirts with Steven Gerrard. It was a great night, and I proved at Albion that I could score goals in the top flight. I got fourteen that season and we managed to avoid relegation. I scored against Arsenal, and we drew. I scored against Manchester United, and we drew. I got a couple against Southampton and then a hat-trick towards the end of the season against Charlton, which proved to be a big result. I got those hat-trick goals all in about fifteen minutes. It was just fantastic to have added a Premier League hat-trick to my collection.

But in the end I became frustrated. I started a lot of games but there were also a lot where I was on the bench and in January 2006 I had the chance to join Norwich, back in the Championship. I really loved it at Carrow Road. I had a year and a half again, and during that one full season I had with the Canaries, I'd got seventeen goals by Christmas. Then I was injured and was out for months. I was gutted because at the time I felt I could have gone on and maybe broken scoring records there, too. But then Derby County, who had just been promoted to the Premier League, came in for me, and I was on my travels again. To say this move was a non-starter is an understatement. There was a massive power-struggle going on behind the scenes when I got there and it became clear early on that I shouldn't be there. I'd come as part of a business deal, I believe, not a football deal. I knew I had to get out and so I made the short move to Nottingham Forest.

It was a great one to make. I wanted to be part of a club that was looking to build something, and that was the case at the City Ground. During the first season, the team struggled to win games although we played well and learned a lot. So much so, we reached the play-offs in the second season, and then again last time out. Some very good players came in and some also came up through the ranks and I got to play up front with Andy Cole, another really top player who'd done it all and was still going strong. In the end, we were very unlucky not to go up after two play-off campaigns. But we'd turned the club around, and I'm proud to have been part of that.

Chapter Thirteen

WHAT HAVE YOU DONE, EARN?

My involvement with Wales has given me some of the proudest moments of my career. It's been an honour to pull on the red shirt, yet it might have all been very different.

The first time I became aware that there could be an international career out there for me was as I was breaking through into the Bluebirds team, and had played a few games in the FAW Cup. People were starting to take notice, and Bobby Gould, the Wales boss at the time, paid me a visit. The first I knew about it was after training one day. I was told the boss wanted to see me and my immediate reaction, as you'd expect at that age, was: "What have I done wrong?" But when I went in to the office I was told Bobby Gould was waiting to see me. Now remember, I was sixteen at the time and only just on the edge of any sort of career with Cardiff City. I thought, wow, the manager of Wales has come to see me? That's crazy! But he sat down with me and asked me what I thought about international football. He made it clear he wanted me to play for Wales but understood I was born in Zambia. Even though I'd spent my formative years in Wales, I always thought that if I was lucky enough to play for my country, that country would be Zambia. My uncle had played for Zambia, and I wanted to represent the country of my birth. But at the same time, there were a few occasions when I went to the old Arms Park to watch Wales, and I just thought how amazing those games were and how lucky the players were to play in them. You've got to remember that I was watching Ian Rush and Ryan Giggs, who had come through. There was Gary Speed emerging on to the scene, too. Wales had some massive names and to be honest in the end that swayed me. But at the time, when Bobby put me on the spot and said he wanted me to play for Wales under-16s, I turned him down. I didn't rule it out, I just wasn't sure what to do. I wasn't ready to make a decision like that. I didn't play at under-16 level at all, but as time moved on, and I was getting a few games for the Cardiff first team, I was beginning to get my head around what to do. I was invited to play for the Wales under-18s, a few people at Ninian Park said I should give it a try and I decided, yes, I want to play for Wales. Besides the possibility of playing in that magnificent stadium alongside so many top players, playing for Zambia was clouded by complications. For starters, I'd be classed as foreigner if I played for Zambia. There was also the issue of the distance to travel. It would impact significantly on my club career. But what mattered more than anything was that I realised I wanted to represent Wales more than Zambia. Wales was the country I wanted to play for above any other. It just took a while to figure this out. And as soon as I started turning out for the under-18s, I thought to myself: "This feels right." I loved it. Eventually I moved up to the under-21s, played a fair few games and then came my debut, which was to be against Germany, in May 2002. If I'd had any doubts in the back of my mind about my decision, this game blew them all away. I was making my debut, against one of the strongest international sides in the world, at the Millennium Stadium. And what's more, the game went like a perfect dream. I scored, beating Oliver Khan, one of the finest goalkeepers of his or probably any generation, and was named man of the match. On the night, I'd just been so up for it. I remember straightaway in the game going on a run, beating a couple of people just to get myself pumped up and into it. It was a perfect occasion.

The Wales boss, Mark Hughes, had put his faith in me and I was determined to repay it. The game flew by and after we'd won, I came off the pitch and I literally couldn't believe it. I've been lucky enough to achieve a fair bit in the game but this just blew everything away, it topped the lot. I remember after the game, with it being a night match we left the stadium about 11 or midnight and I went back to my house. My mate James Collins came back with me to chill out really but I was just buzzing, I was stunned. There was no way either us was going to sleep. So for hours, literally until about 5 a.m., me and 'Ginge' just sat on my bed, staring into space, too shocked to take it all in. Every now and again, James would say: "What have you done, Earn?" Then it would be: "Have you just scored the winner against Germany?" It just didn't seem real, it seemed impossible and we both felt the same way. Then I'd say: "What have I done, Ginge?" He'd reply, "Yeh, what have you done, Earn?" I'll remember sitting there on the end of my old bed forever, me and Ginge, two kids from Cardiff City, trying to get our heads round beating Germany, with Oliver Khan, Christian Ziege, loads of top players. I couldn't stop thinking: "What has just happened?" Eventually, tiredness broke the spell and we got some sleep. Ginge stayed over and both of us then woke up mid-morning hungry, and there was an Asda just down the road from my house at the time, in Caerphilly. We went to Asda but decided to have a breakfast in the cafe rather than take anything back home, so there we were, the pair of us tucking into an Asda fry-up. And as soon as we sat down, people were coming up to us, asking for autographs, asking if they could have a picture with us. It was constant. I'd scored a lot of goals for Cardiff City and was used to getting recognised but this was completely different. Loads of people were coming up to me! Everybody knew that I'd scored against Germany. It was a great feeling, although I think my breakfast probably ended up cold! As we sat there and people came up, I turned back to James and said, "What have I done, Ginge?" And so we started off again! Well, eventually it sank in and I went on to play a fair few games, I played well and was involved. I scored a few goals and then in February 2004 came another fantastic occasion in my career so far, in a friendly game against Scotland, again at the Millennium Stadium. I had a feeling beforehand that this game was going to be a great one for me and when I scored early on, I think in the first five minutes or so, I got other chances and scored a hat-trick. This was my international hat-trick, and it's one of a complete set of hat-tricks, scored at every professional division and in all the Cup competitions. We won the game 4–0 and it wasn't a meaningless friendly, far from it. At the time, there hadn't been so many matches between the so-called 'home' nations and it wasn't a game with a dozen substitutions, or anything like that. We wanted to win, so did they and there was a big crowd in the Millennium Stadium. To get the hat-trick blew me away all over again, it was just brilliant and the fans' reaction was so special. At the time, the team had been together for two or three years. We'd gone very, very close to qualifying for Euro 2004, we'd narrowly lost a play-off against Russia and there were some decent players emerging for Wales. One other wonderful benefit from my time with Wales is being in the same team as Giggsy. I remember when I was still just an under-21, we stayed in the same hotels as the senior team for trips away and I was blown away when I'd see Ryan in the corridor. I wanted to ask for his autograph. I probably still do! Ryan made such an impact on me when I was learning the game myself, he was a huge hero of mine and he still is an inspiration for me. I remember how embarrassed I felt when I got a similar cheer to him when my name was read out ahead of a game at the Millennium Stadium. It just didn't feel right! Just watching him in training, his technique, his close control, it's been such an education and I think from just watching him it's helped me improve as a player. So mixing with Ryan, my big football hero, has been a dream come true. But things have been very up and down since the middle of the last decade, and the last five years in particular. Mark Hughes moved on to club management and then John Toshack came in. I have to say that I feel during this time, Wales as a national side came to a standstill. Things were stuck in neutral for far too long.

At the time of writing I have only just learned of the tragic news of Gary Speed's death. Gary had of course come in as permanent successor to John Toshack and our performances and results had certainly picked up. But in late November we lost our manager, leader and a great person who had inspired us during his time in charge. He had introduced a completely different philosophy for us. For many reasons, we now must try and honour his memory by carrying on the good work that he started and continue to improve over the next few years.

As our manager, Gary's attention to detail was amazing. Everything was examined in detail: where people should be; when they should be there; the space people should be moving in to. We adopted a 'thinking' philosophy. How do we beat a team? How do we get space? It has benefited me, not least because I enjoyed working with Gary from the minute he arrived.

Perhaps it had only been the last six months or so that results started to improve but you've got to remember that the Wales squad might only be together for a handful of weeks every year. It takes time to get a message, a new way of thinking, across to a group of players who get together so infrequently. Everything Gary introduced was so professional. The Welsh team has become like a top club set-up and it would be great if that can continue. Not many sides in the Premier League have been doing what we've been doing. There's a lot of recovery stuff, aimed at conditioning. It's been about the best possible preparation, taking a really close look at the opposition, planning how best to exploit their weaknesses.

For me, it has been completely the opposite to how it was under John Toshack. I don't feel we had a direction with Tosh as boss. We didn't have a focus. Gary brought in a clear goal, to qualify for a major tournament. It would now be wonderful if we could achieve that goal in Gary's memory. Previously, before Gary came in, the attitude seemed to be that we might be happy with a draw. We might be happy to just be out there, and aiming to not lose if we could avoid it. It wasn't the right set-up. But I feel we have started growing as a team again. We've had some fantastic talent coming through in the past five or six years and although it has taken time, and will take more time again and luck with injuries, we have been heading in the right direction. Before, results were patchy, players always seemed to be retiring or falling out with the manager. Now, we have a clear aim, and we also want to be the best Wales team we can be. We want to entertain.

Over the last few years, Barcelona, for me, have completely changed the way people think about football and have shown that you can play a beautiful, flowing, passing game, you can stick to these principles and still be head and shoulders above everyone else. I'm not trying to say that the Wales team can be like Barcelona but we can learn from their principles. We don't want to just kick the ball long and hope for the best, as has happened in the past. We want to entertain. We want to play the game as it should be played. At the same time, we want to finally reach a major tournament and if we don't do that, for whatever reason, we want to make sure we all enjoy the ride and learn from any mistakes to make sure we do realise this dream.

Chapter Fourteen

COMING HOME AND THE FUTURE

YOU might think it was a 'no brainer' for me to come back to Cardiff when the opportunity arose during last summer. It wasn't quite that simple. For me, when it comes to making big decisions like this I want to try and detach myself from the emotions involved and be sure, in my own mind, that I'm doing something for the right reasons. In the end, what convinced me that coming home to Cardiff was right was the possibility of being involved in getting the club into the Premier League. I should, touch wood, be here for the rest of this season, next season and possibly a third season. We will see what happens beyond that. Obviously, Cardiff is home to me but the whole process of coming back took a while. I knew from more than a year ago, from July 2010, that I had one year left on my contract. Nottingham Forest were interested in convincing me to stay and I thought, no problem, I'm enjoying my time at Forest. I enjoyed the club, being part of the team. It's a big, big club with a massive history. But time started to tick down. I had seven months left, then six, five. Put it this way, Forest were not making me an offer I couldn't refuse! I wanted to stay, but negotiations on a new deal weren't going very well. So I stepped in and told the club to leave it a few months, to come back to it and I'd just focus on playing football. I didn't need it going on in the background. But we got well into the New Year, and things were just a little bit too quiet for my liking. From January, I was in a position where I could talk with other clubs, but as the end of the season came into view, and we were pushing for a place in the Premier League via the play-offs, I just thought I'm not going to sign anything right now. Let's get my head down, try and help the club get promoted and take it from there. But we were beaten over two legs in the play-off semi-finals by Swansea City, and then the manager, Billy Davies, didn't know what was happening, if I was staying or going. I was starting to get mixed signals. I think the will was there to keep me, but they were making it harder than it should have been. It was all too cool, too distant. The chairman, Nigel Doughty, was one of the people who really wanted to keep me at the club. He's a great guy, his son plays for Wales at youth level, and he had always taken a big interest in me. But other issues, like budgets for example, were obstacles and my attitude was, if they want to keep me, they'll find a way. It came down to the end of my contract, and there was contact from Cardiff City, nothing formal, just contact. They definitely wanted me, but there was a lot going on at the time, with the managerial situation – regarding Dave Jones's future – still up in the air. It came to June and we just thought we'd go on holiday, not worry about it. At this time, I was getting offers from all over the world. There were possibilities in the US, in China, in Qatar. There was interest in Turkey, as well as a lot from here. There were a number of clubs in Britain keen to speak to me. I really had a lot to think about when I got back from my break. I wanted to take my time to get the decision right, and make sure I was making it for the right reasons. The managerial situation at Cardiff was clarified with Malky Mackay coming in, and he made David Kerslake, a guy I'd worked with at Forest, his assistant. The club was in a better place than when I'd left. The stadium, the training ground, it is all set up for making the next step. I had to decide where would I play my best football and be most comfortable. I had always hoped I'd get another chance to play for Cardiff. I wanted to come home, be back with my family just down the road, with them all coming to watch me. I want my little boy, Silva, to grow up here watching me playing for Cardiff. I love the place, it's such a great city and place to live. But the football side had to be right, I had to be at a club which had ambition. I want to play in the Premier League again if possible. In the end, coming home did tick all the boxes. So much had changed at Cardiff City while I'd been away, but it was still the same club deep down, still the same fans. While I'd been away, whenever I'd played for another club against Cardiff, the fans here had been so good to me. I remember when I was playing for Norwich, I scored against Cardiff and the fans just clapped! A lot of fans can be ruthless when you leave, they forget the time you've spent with them, but not City fans. All they wanted to do was applaud me, sing for me to do the Ayatollah. It was like, they were thinking it's OK. It's Earnie, he's one of us. These are the same people who supported me when I was 16. They're great and I'll always appreciate how good they've been to me. And when I came back, during the pre-season games, I came across some of the faces who'd been there at the start of my career. It was like I'd never been away. So hopefully, I can be here a few years and we can all enjoy the ride. And I definitely want to play on for as long as I can. I've played with some great players who were 37, or 38. Look at Ryan Giggs. So if I can have another eight or so years, and be part of getting Cardiff City into the Premier League, where the club would grow so much bigger again, then I'd be absolutely thrilled. But in the meantime, I'll try to keep on scoring the goals, and with any luck, you might still be seeing me doing the somersaults on a pitch not too far away for a good many years yet!

Quick Reads 📖

Fall in love with reading

Going for Gold

Accent Press

What does it take to go for gold and be the greatest?

In *Going For Gold*, Wales's leading athletes share the secrets of their drive and determination to be the best in their sport.

Cyclist Geraint Thomas, who won Olympic gold in the Team Pursuit in Beijing 2008, and 11 times gold medal-winning paralympic swimmer Dave Roberts talk of their ambitions to win in London 2012.

World champion hurdler David 'Dai' Greene explains his hunger to be the best and the importance of loving what you do, while Commonwealth medal-winning swimmer Jazmin 'Jazz' Carlin and paralympic world champion Nathan Stephens reveal the discipline needed to go for gold.

This collection of stories will inspire others to aim for their goals and follow their dreams.

Quick Reads

Fall in love with reading

Why do Golf Balls have Dimples?
Wendy Sadler

Accent Press

Have you ever wondered why golf balls have dimples or why your hair goes frizzy in the rain? Scientist Wendy Sadler has the answers in her book of Weird and Wonderful facts.

Broken down into user-friendly chapters like sport, going out, the great outdoors, food and drink and the downright weird, Wendy's book gives the scientific answers to life's intriguing questions, like why toast always lands butter-side down and why you can't get (too) lost with a satnav.

Quick Reads 📖

Fall in love with reading

Finger Food
Helen Lederer

Accent Press

Bella le Pard's career as a TV presenter is 'on hold'. To fill her days, she sits in a coffee shop and obsesses about a wedding dress in the neighbouring shop. Her luck changes when she gets the call from her old boss at 'Flair for living TV' to present a pilot for a new food and chat show. But her revived TV career is short-lived when one of the celebrity guests threatens to steal the show. Bella finds herself turning to blackmail to save her job. But will her threat to reveal her boss's infidelity keep her on TV? And will she ever find a reason to buy that dream wedding dress?

This comedy from one of the UK's best-loved funny ladies will make you laugh out loud.

About the Author

Known to the fans as 'Earnie', Robert Earnshaw is one of Cardiff City's top scorers. Born in Mufulira, Zambia, he moved to Bedwas in south Wales with his Welsh mother in 1985. He began his professional career with Cardiff City in 1998. During his first spell at Cardiff he scored 105 goals. He made his international debut for Wales in 2002. Moving up the divisions Earnie became Premier League side West Bromwich Albion's top scorer before signing for Norwich City, Derby County and then Nottingham Forest. In 2011 he returned to Cardiff City.